Fabulous Faith

in

Meet My Worry Monster

by Melissa Webster

Illustrations by Lili Lapellegrina
Book and cover design by Sarah E. Holroyd (http://sleepingcatbooks.com)

ISBN: 978-1-5239-6046-0

To the loves of my life, James and Lilyanna Faith.

Thank you for making my world a better place by just being you. God blessed me beyond measure.

Lilyanna, keep being the light. Mommy and Daddy are so proud of you.

Thank you, Britney Yanucci, for your guidance and for teaching us bubble breathing.

This is me. My name is Faith. I am super fabulous and I love to play and do many new things.

This is my worry monster. He is super stinky and he loves to try to stop me from doing the things that I love.

This is my school. It has great teachers, fun things to play with, and it even has two Guinea pigs named Milk and Cookies.

It also has my friend Alan who cracks me up. One day he made me laugh so hard my chocolate milk went through my nose (gross, I know).

Note to self: don't drink chocolate milk when playing with Alan.

This is my mom and dad. They are so much fun, except when they say it's time for bed. Boohoo!

Here is my dog Alfie. He loves to lick your face. Eww, doggy breath!

Don't tell him he has doggy breath though, that wouldn't be polite.

I also have a fish that I feed every day. Mom says I am learning to be responsible.

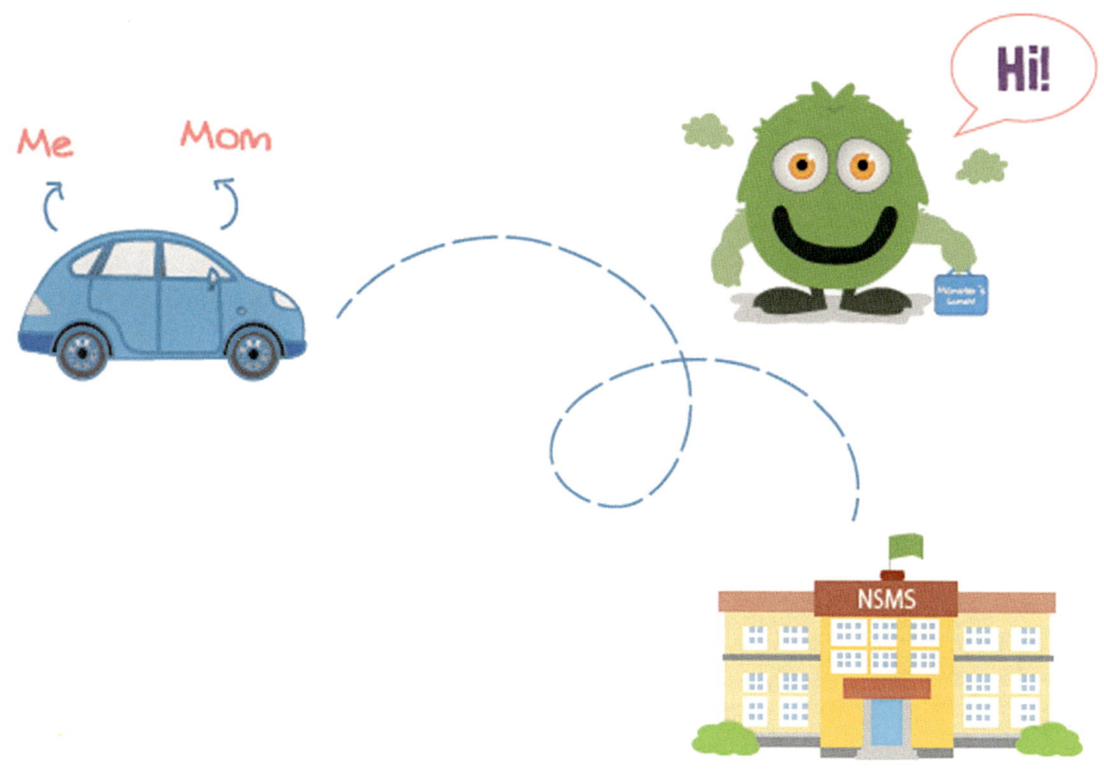

My mom drove me to school and that was the first time I met my worry monster, Stan.

I did not know it was him at first,
but here is what happened...

I started to think:

Then my tummy started feeling funny. It felt like I had butterflies all over my heart. My face started to feel red like a tomato. And I just started crying and decided right then and there I did not like school and I would not go anymore.

My mom tried to tell me about all the fun I would have, that she always comes back and she would never leave me.

But stinky Stan told me not to believe her and I just cried and screamed. I didn't even really hear my mom, only Stan. I said, "I am not going. I can't go."

But guess what happened next...

I still had to go to school, kicking and screaming. (FYI, kids' school is not an option.)

My worry monster took over. I couldn't stop him. I thought to myself, "I just want to go home."

Guess what? After my mom left, Fabulous Faith conquered stinky Stan.

I remembered what my mom and dad always told me. They told me how we all have this super power to control our thoughts. It is the greatest thing.

I think my super power looks like this. Well that's what I think anyway.

You see, I had the power all along. With a few deep breaths in and out from my belly, stinky Stan started to shrink a bit.

Then I said to myself, "My mom always comes back. You are a liar, Stan. She always comes back."

Then he got even smaller.

I pictured in my head my mom walking through the doors of school. I saw us hugging and going home to our after-school hot cocoa date.

But stan did not give up and started making me feel like I should worry about being at school.

I told Stan, "That is a lie, Stan. My mom would never forget about me. You are stinky and I have a super power to defeat you. So you have to go."

Then I stomped him out. I pictured it in my head like this.

He got super small then.

I remembered how my mom said the trick to make any day go faster is to get busy. So I found my friend Alan and said, "Let's go build a castle."

Next thing you know, I was having so much fun with my friends at lunch and it was almost time to go home.

I looked at the clock and Stinky Stan started to creep in, saying, "Your mommy won't come back, ha ha ha!"

I took a deep breath and said to myself, "Go away, Stan, you stink. My mom always comes back."

He got smaller again.

We went back to my classroom for circle time.

My teacher, Mrs. Applebottom, told us the most interesting facts about kangaroos. I love kangaroos. They live in Australia. I love Austraila.

Then before I knew it, we were lining up to go home and there was my mom.

Stan was defeated.

See, Stinky Stan. I knew you were lying.

The next day on the way to school Stan came back AGAIN. Can you believe him? I would not let him win!

I remembered my super power to control my thoughts. It was in me all along and I can always use it.

The less I listen to Stan and the more I listen to myself, the less he comes around. The more I get busy doing something I love, the less Stan bothers me.

So get busy at school, join in and play. Talk to your teachers. You can tell them you are feeling worried and they can help you too.

But really the power is in you. Tell your worry monster to beat it and you will win. Just like me!

Here's what you can do. Draw a picture of your worry monster.

Give your worry monster a name:

Remember these affirmations.
(You say that word like this: A-FUR-MATION.)

* God is with me
* My mom and dad always come back
* I am safe
* I love my school
* I love my friends
* I am strong
* I am brave
* I've got this
* Just because I think it, doesn't mean I believe it
* I can do anything
* Write your own:

____

____

Remember, the power is in you. You can always control your thoughts, and that will always make you feel better.

About the author

Melissa currently lives in Patchogue, New York, with her husband, James, five-year-old daughter, Lilyanna, and their dog (furbaby), Alfie. Melissa enjoys spending time with her family at the beach, boating, and traveling. In her spare time, Melissa is an active member of her church as a catechist coordinator and alpha host. She is a wish granter for the Make-A-Wish Foundation in Suffolk County and sits on various charity committees. She has a passion for children's literature. Mostly she loves being a stay-at-home mother and wife.

When Lilyanna began preschool, like most children she endured separation anxiety. Melissa read every book on the subject and sought professional advice to help her daughter with the transition. It was a very trying and upsetting time for everyone. Melissa soon discovered that most of the books did not address the fact that the anxiety resurfaces for the child throughout their day at school, and continues the next day, sometimes for weeks. Melissa wanted Lilyanna to learn to use her own skills to control these anxious thoughts, and not allow them to roil around in her mind. Thus *Fabulous Faith in Meet My Worry Monster* was born. It is written from the child's perspective and is presented in a cute, funny, and empowering way for children and adults.

Made in the USA
Coppell, TX
13 June 2024

33461752R00021